JOBY, UNINTERRUPTED--
BITTERSWEET SYMPHONIES AND BOHEMIAN RHAPSODIES
(1989-2009)

JOBY, UNINTERRUPTED--
BITTERSWEET SYMPHONIES
AND BOHEMIAN RHAPSODIES
(1989-2009)

Joseph Powell

ISBN 978-0-557-10424-6

for Toni & Santi
and my mama
and to the memory of
James Baldwin
and Langston Hughes
and to all the poets
who have blazed the path
for me to do what I do

Contents

The Negro Speaks Of Langston Hughes

I've known the blues;
The eternal tom-tom of joy and laughter;
Pain swallowed in a smile.

I know, because of Langston;
His words drunk deep into my soul,
Like fine cherry wine;
Words which flow down like waters
Into the wellspring of my being;
Flows like the blood
That courses through my veins.

I've known jazz;
The sound of the "A" train racing to Harlem;
The heartbreak of Lady Day;
The za-ba-doo-bop of Satchmo.

I've known blackness,
Because of Langston—
Of what happens to a dream deferred;
Of cotton fields and the Mississippi;
Of spirituals and folksongs;
Of beauty and ugliness.

I know of poetry,
Because of Langston—
For you can't be black and a poet,
And not give the man his due.

I know
When the Negro speaks of Langston,
He speaks of America;
Of black folks

And white folks;
And even the brown, yellow,
And red folks;
When the Negro speaks of Langston,
He speaks of himself.

Floating Up A Stream Of Consicousness Without A Paddle

I would like to say something important
Before I die and am buried
Six feet under and my soul is carried
Off to heaven and my name
Becomes a mere memory to
A select few people, who may or
May not have wept at my funeral.
But what should I say? I don't know—
What would you like to hear? Should
It be witty or perverted or morbid?
Should I say it in 25 words or less, or
Shall I speak as if I'm answering an essay
Question? Should I wax eloquent about
The meaning of life; ruminate
About what I consider to exist beyond
The cosmos; shall I pontificate
On the wonders of the supernatural and
All things theological? Should I
Ask how do I love thee, and then
Count the ways which are beyond numeration?
Should I speak in sentences or
Kindergarten gibberish, which would be
Rather interesting, considering
The wisdom that comes from the mouths of babes?
Shall I opine about the nature of the human condition;
Editorialize on the state of race relations
In this country—what it means
To be black in white America, to be
A stranger in a strange land, an
Alien on foreign shores, still
Trying to find his place in society, his
Niche in the vast scheme of things?

Or shall I enunciate about what I
Appreciate about the concept of love—
Whatever the hell it is? Shall I
Discuss, such as they are, my
Inadequacies and shortcomings, faults and
Misgivings, the ugliness and
The pain; perhaps express the
Joys and triumphs and even small victories
Won? Or should I just shut up, say
Nothing, live out my raison d'etre, die
In peace, and close this damn
Poem?

Neapolitan Baby

(for Josie)

The black was for you
The white was for me
The pink was a bonus
Or a symbol that
She was just a little girl
In a feline body

But she was our queen—
Fierce in her independence,
Sweet in her innocence;
She could warm a heart
Or tickle you silly,
With her playfulness

It didn't take three years
To fall in love with her;
But three years isn't a life,
Not even for a cat.
But you said that maybe
They needed a black
And white one up in heaven.

And I guess that will have
To be enough for me,
Save,
For this one prayer—

Lord, take care of Josie;
Give her a warm spot to lay
And plenty of room to play;
A couple of mice wouldn't hurt,

Even if they're toy ones;
Keep her company
Til we get there.

Amen.

Resolved: To Be Seen and Heard

(An Invisible Man Speaks Out)

Hear me, America!
For I will not be silent.
I will not go gentle
Into that good night
Or anywhere else you wish me to go.
For I am here
And here I'll stay,
Until you acknowledge me
Or die trying.
For I am your darker brother
You'd rather keep in the closet;
The invisible man you choose not to see;
The millionth man wishing to be counted;
The rapper and the preacher,
Speaking the truth to you in love,
But by all means necessary.

I am the somebody standing next to you in an elevator,
As you clutch your purse tighter and hope that
I'm not getting off on the same floor as you.
I am God's child, sitting next to you in church,
And yet as far away from you as the east is from the west.

I am the one who got away
From the projects, drugs, gangs, and prisons;
Who works on Wall Street, Madison Ave, the Wilshire District,
and the Magnificent Mile;
But can't catch a cab or buy a home
or get a loan or date your daughter
or live next door to you.

I am Othello, the hero you love in public,
and the scourge you hate in private.
I am James Baldwin,
Malcolm X,
Martin Luther King,
Thurgood Marshall,
Langston Hughes,
W.E.B. DuBois,
And a host of others--
Still wondering, when are you going to wake up?
Wondering, when are you going to get it?

I am the ghost of decades past;
Of slavery and lynchings,
Of white sheets and burning crosses,
Of Jim Crow and "Move to the rear",
Of attack dogs and fire hoses,
Of "Wait!" and "Be patient!",
Of assassinations and wiretaps,
Of getting the mule without the 40 acres,
Of affirmative action and Indian-giving
(If you know what I mean!).

Am I bugging you?
Have I got under your skin?
Because you haven't gotten under mine yet,
Nor have you walked in my shoes.
For if you could, you'd see
That I am you and you are me;
The reflection of your hopes and fears,
Your thoughts and dreams;
The other side of the coin;
Truth staring you in the face;
Love waiting to be received;
The dream tired of being deferred;
The voice in the wilderness,
waiting to be answered.

Will you see me as I am,

Not as what pride and prejudice
Has blinded you to?
Will you hear me
Amidst the din and noise
Of fear and ignorance?
Hear me say,
In a still small voice,
"I love you!"........

I'm still waiting.

Face

(for Toni)

The sun rises
Just to greet your smile
And the stars
In the night sky
Want to know
How you make your eyes sparkle;

Me,
I'm wanting to know
How I came to deserve
Such beauty.

Blood On The Page

Sitting here, trying to bleed on the page
Can't find a vein
My pen's getting duller by the minute
So I stick it down my throat,
Hoping something 'll come that way
But all I get are dry heaves,
Fits and starts, monosyllables
And half-baked images,
Not fully digested.

It's a bitch to be a poet;
An unemployed one at that;
Instead of looking for words,
I'm looking for a job
And feeling like Job,
Arguing with God
In the whirlwind;
Feeling,
Like Christ on the cross,
Asking why me?
Why have you forsaken me?

To All The Brothers Who Ain't Here

To all the brothers who ain't here
Gone too soon
Voices still needed
Stories left untold
Songs still unsung
Victories left unwon.
Where have you gone?
I wish you'd return
For who will fill the empty spaces?
Who will give names to the faces?
Who will speak the truth not spoken?
Who will scream of laws gone broken?
Of dreams deferred
And plans deterred.
Welfare mothers
And absent fathers;
Gangbanging sons
And pregnant daughters;
Brothers on crack
And sisters in the street;
For those of us still tired and poor
In huddled masses
Yearning to breathe free.

O tell us brothers
Who will speak now?
Who will sing?
Who will scribble
The jots and tittles
Depicting blood and spittle
Of bodies broken and souls crushed
Under the weight of unfulfilled promises

And politically correct lies?
Who will weed out the beatific
From the bullshit?
Who will be our prophets, our poets,
Our dreamkeepers and truthsayers?
Though your shoes, I cannot fill,
And your pen, I cannot hold,
Yet here I am
Ready to be commissioned
If you deem me worthy.
May I see visions
And proclaim boldly
And write honestly.
May my words, sewn together,
Become tapestries,
Not only capturing your memory,
But stitching together
Our history
And illuminating our mystery.

Tears Like Drops Of Blood

Is it possible to scream in a crowded mall
and have no one hear you?
Well, I didn't exactly scream, but the tears
Were real.
And I've sworn to myself that I would
Never weep in public.
But this time, it was personal.
This was no boy crying wolf,
This was a man shedding real tears,
Falling down like drops of blood.
And I was weeping for those no longer here:

For England and their lost rose;
For India's children and their mother superior;
For a community of poets still howling in remorse,
Eating naked lunches and yet still going hungry;

I wept for the Farleys and for the
Dangerous paths comics choose to tread;
And for the Kennedys, my God,
What they've endured.
And can you believe that Cher still
Loved Sonny after all these years?

I wept for Bedford Falls and the loss of their native son;
For Bill and Camille,
Who lost their only begotten son;
For the ordinary and courageous
Who've lost their gravelly-voiced spokesperson;

I wept for the Middle East,
Where there may never be peace;

I wept for Bosnia,
Where they're still searching for hope
Among the ruins;
And yes, I even wept for myself,
For yes, Virginia,
Real men do cry, damn it,
And should never be ashamed.

I wept for the times I've been misunderstood;
For being lonely and afraid;
For wanting to love and sometimes
Not being able to do so;
For missed opportunities and
Mistakes avoidable and not;
For words that should've been put down
On paper and spoken aloud,
But are now lost to the four winds,
Never to be recaptured.

And I wept for the people in the mall
As they walked by,
Weeping for their pains and their sorrows;
Wondering where they may find themselves alone,
In a crowded mall,
Weeping aloud,
And might they weep for me
As I walk by.

Sister Friend

(dedicated to Mary and Rhona)

Was it five years ago
When I first called you friend;
We entered into sisterhood
To last till the end
Of time.
Til death do us part,
We hold each other's heart;
Deepest secrets do we share,
Girlish laughter fills the air,
Like rain.
When teardrops fall, they remind us of
The pain
We've both known and endured—
Allowing grace, so amazing and secure
To keep us going, ever growing
Closer and closer;
Held together
By the tie that binds.

Will we last another five, ten,
Fifteen, twenty years?
Are you kidding?
Give up late night raps
And Sunday noon naps;
Of fighting and bitching,
But once again ditching
Another pointless argument
For an umpteenth hug
Or a Coke and a smile?!

Sister, oh dear sister friend,
How do I love thee?
Yea, how do I need thee!
Will you stay my forever friend?
'Cause God brought us together
To endure any weather;
The storminess of loneliness
That being sisters has erased
Like the sunshine after the rain.

So let's walk down that road
Carrying each other's load
Til we reach our final destination—
The ultimate culmination
Of our hugs and smiles,
Laughter and tears,
Borne through the living years—
Heaven!
Singing glory hallelujah,
We have made it, sister friend!

Ode To A Love I Never Had

Like a distant memory,
She comes to me in a vision;
Vague,
Like a hologram,
Fading in and out.
Did I know you in another life?
Or was it just yesterday
That I held you in my arms,
Caressing you like a lover?
Or was I protecting you , like a little girl?
Touching your lips, but not to mine;
Easing the pain that stabbed your brain,
Wanting you to know that everything would
Be alright.

You haunt me like a well-remembered melody,
With a well-forgotten name.
Holding in your hands
That which I knew I had lost some time ago.
Haunting me, taunting me
Laughing at me with the laugh
You used to share with me at a joke
We both once loved—do you remember it?
Neither do I, except
You left me standing by the side of the road,
In front of an old grey house
With all the lights turned out
When I wanted to give you the moon
So that you could swallow it, see,
And the moonbeams would shoot out
Through the ends of your hair
And to the tips of your toes

And, and…
Am I talking too much?

Odd, for a man with a hole in his soul
And no place to go, but back to the future,
Where I sit writing this poem
And wondering why I have a headache
That feels like a steam train?
And what was I talking about anyway?
I can't remember; all I keep hearing is
That crazy laugh without a joke and
Remembering those soft hands
With the Palmolive touch,
Enveloping that which I'd sworn
Was yours to keep—
Haunting me, taunting me;
But now all I want from you is,
All you can do for me is,
Give me back my heart, please,
Give me back my heart.

A World In Your Eye

(dedicated to Alice Walker and my mother)

I see a world in your eye, Mama,
Though that eye cannot see—
I see the pain and the suffering,
The trials and the triumphs,
The joys and the sorrows,
The todays and tomorrows;
I see the loves and the heartaches,
The sunshine as the day breaks.

I see the healing power of laughter
And the killing power of hatred.
I see black and white in a grey world.
I see stories told and retold, and even
Some stories untold.
I see the color purple
And children in search of their mothers'
gardens.
I see the forests and the trees,
The birds and the bees;
I see the rivers and the streams
And a host of people's dreams.

I see the apocalypse, the end of the rainbow,
The Alpha and the Omega;
I see the end of the world in your eye, Mama,
Though that eye cannot see.

Memento

Your taste in my mouth
Sustains me;
Fills me with thoughts
Of yesterdays
Spent walking the beach;
Of dancing naked
Under the stars;
Making love to the music
Of Bird and Miles,
Wishing this moment was
Forever
And waking up to
The sound of reality
Clothed in the raindrops
That fall outside
And the realization
In my head
And my broken heart
That all I have left
Of you is
Your taste in my mouth.

Season Of The Poem

Cut my finger on a razor blade
My baby just ran out of Kool-Aid
And I'm still waiting to get paid,
Or laid, which is better
When it's wetter.
It's the season of the poem.
Don't mind me
Or try to find me
Lost in a haze
Gone for days
(or however long it takes
to finish this poem)
this poem is wack,
but not for lack

of rhyme or reason—
It's the season
Of the poem;
Of speaking the truth, Ruth,
And making it plain, Jane;
Of exchanging words
For gunfire;
Love for hire,
But not what you're thinking;
Cause this ship is sinking
And we ain't even hit the iceburg
Yet.

But I'll tell you this,
Ignorance ain't bliss
When Freddy got fingered
At the box office

And Survivor's #1
And we're still asking
Why Johnny can't read.

When a somebody can get
Pulled over
For driving while black;
And white is still
Considered right;
And gay can get you killed;
And you need a pill to get it up;
And you need money to get money
Or votes or…
Pardon me—
I know I'm getting off
On a rant here
(sorry Dennis),
but it's enough to make a
man holler, the way
they do our life
(thanks Marvin).
And I'm sitting here trying
To finish this poem
And I'm thinking of Leonard
And Mumia rotting in jail
And at least Charlie Manson
Gets a parole hearing
(and a website!);

And Amadou, poor Amadou—
Public Enemy said it would
Take a nation of millions
To hold us back,
And it took 41 shots
To bring you down
And I wonder what
Was in that wallet
You pulled.

And I better stop here
Before I drop tears
And run out of words
Cause there are more poems to write
And time to call it a night.
Tomorrow is another day
And I will have more to say.

Peace.

Sleeps In Shadow

She sleeps in shadow
Bad dreams
Sometimes haunt her,
Coming,
In the middle of the night
Like a thief;
And I ,
Lying next to her,
Forever the poet,
Trying to conjure up words
That will comfort her
In the darkness
As I try to keep
My own bad dreams
At bay.

She

(inspired by Lord Byron)

She talks
To me
In poetry
In still small voices
And seductive whispers
And speaks to me
Of eternal life
And love unending
Her tone never wavers
But resonates,
Soothingly,
Giving me chills,
Caressing my body,
Calming my soul.

She looks
At me
With eyes so fair
And unrelenting
She
Of the tender eyes
And darkest hair
She
Of the rosy lips
And warmest smile
She
Who can caress
With one look,
One touch,
One word.
She

Of the giving heart
And sweet embrace.
She
Second to angels
Made in the image of God
For God too is beautiful.
She
Who walks in beauty
Like the night
And stirs men’s souls to song.
She
The rarest find
The precious pearl
She
Who’s touched me to the very core
She
Who walks in beauty
She who walks
She who
She.

If

If I told you, you had a nice body,
Would you hold it against me?
If I stared into your eyes so blue,
Said, 'I love you',
And promised you the moon,
Would you believe me?

If I gave you my heart,
The very best part;
If I said, you were the only one,
Brighter than the sun,
My Eden,
Would you let me in?

If I whispered your name,
If tomorrow never came,
If I bathed you in flowers,
Made love to you for hours,
Would you give me tonight?

If you feel my confidence is sure,
And you know your longing is pure;
If we never did another thing,
But simply made each other sing,
Would you take a chance?

At Play In The Fields Of Blood

Our playgrounds have become battlefields
Monkey bars, slides, and sand boxes—
Caked in blood,
The blood of children;
Innocence shattered
Like a broken mirror;
And it's now seventy times seven
Years of bad luck
For each child.

The children that are our future
Are taking matters into their own hands
In the form of 9 mm's and .38 calibers
That are now available
At your local Toys R' Us.
This isn't child's play,
Nah, this is a new day.
Who wants to be a millionaire?
Sorry Regis,
It's all about Survivor, baby.
Tag, you're dead.
Sticks and stones still break bones
But a bullet hurts forever.

Weakest link, yeah,
I got your weakest link right here;
AK-47, baby, yeah,
When you absolutely, positively,
Gotta kill every...
You know the story.

And we wonder why,
Why?

Ask the President;
Ask Chuck Heston;
Ask the father who
Forgot to lock up
His gun cabinet;
Or the mother
Who thought
The pantry
Was a good hiding place;
Ask yourself.
Before it's too late.
Oops, it is too late.
Game over.
Bang, you're dead!

Apple and Rose

She
Touched me to the very core
Peeling away every layer of my being
To get at part of me she most desired
Seed
The very element of life
That which she would need for her own growth
To bloom, where she was planted
To become,
That which by any other name
Would still smell as sweet.

Dancing With The Devil In The Pale Moonlight

Bats in the belfry
A joker in the deck
Damsel in distress
Gotham City in a wreck
As we dance to the song of a prince.

Souls in conflict
A symbol of good vs. a symbol of evil
A dark knight, a laughing clown
Who will save the people?
As we dance to the song of a prince.

The pale moon glances
At lovers in their trances
At those who take their chances
With passionate romances
Shall we dance to the song of a prince?

As the moon makes its rise
Amidst the glistening skies
I see a man alone, standing in black
All is well in Gotham City
And with a woman sitting pretty
Who dares to fall in love with a bat.

The pale moonlight does funny things to you
When you dance to the song of a prince.
Long may they dance to the song
Of a prince!

Sultry

She says my name
Each time like
It's the first time;
Making love to me
With her voice
Because my body
I wasn't ready to
Let her have,
For it meant losing
Control of something
I was not yet prepared
To give;
And she deserved
Better, oh yes,
She does;
But her voice,
Her voice, which still intoxicates,
And her eyes,
Damn! her eyes,
Which see through
The window of my soul.
Stop staring at me,
For I will lose control
And then there may be
Nothing to stop me.

But if you say my name
And if you say yes
And if you say, "I still want you",
Cause only those words will do;
Then maybe I'll surrender
And maybe I'll say yes

And maybe it'll be magic
Like making love should be;
And then we'll know
And then we'll know
And then we'll know
And it might change things
And it might not,
But c'est la vie
C'est la vie
Say my name
Say my name
Say my name
Say you still want me
Say you still want me
Say you still want me
Say yes
Say yes
Say…
Yes.

Cut

She said,
'I don't think
you love me'.
No dagger was
Made
That cut
As deep.

They say,
'Words can
never hurt
you'.

I say,
Next time,
She should
Use sticks
And
Stones.

A Hymn For Sister Maya

(for Maya Angelou)

The epitome of eloquence,
The embodiment of elegance;
Queen--
Mother Africa descended
In all her glorious splendor.
Her voice,
Once silent long ago,
Now springs forth
Like the thunder
Of a thousand rainstorms
And just as nourishing;
Or,
Like the still small voice
Of a gentle angel,
Bearing glad tidings
Of great joy.
Her beauty
Knows no equal;
Her words
Are like fine silk,
Smooth to the touch,
Pleasing to the skin;

Or,
A double-edged sword
Piercing bone and marrow,
For she can't help
But bring forth truth,
The truth.
It is her gift to us--
Her calling,

Her life's blood,
Her duty
As one raised up from the wilderness,
Not as a reed swayed by the wind,
But a prophetess of the highest order.

She is
That heaven we find in a wildflower,
Our mirror to nature;
But not only that.
She is
The storefront preacher;
The street rapper;
The social worker;
That favorite teacher.
She is
Mother, daughter;
Sister, lover;
Friend;
Our fielder of dreams
And conveyer of nightmares.

She is
The cry of Rachel
Weeping for her children
And refusing to be comforted.
She is
The song of the virgin Mary
In praise to her God.
The world is brighter
Because she has shone her light
In our dark places.
Her candle
Will one day
Blow out,
But the flame
That she has ignited
Will burn on,
Eternal,
For that is

What flames do.

Red Light, Green Light

The girl in the car
next to me
smiles at me
as I wait
for the green
Hoping it'll never
come
As I stare at her
Heart racing
Mind pounding
Wanting to know her name
To kiss her lips
To...
There's the green
And her car takes off
As she waves
And I follow after
Hoping for
the next
Red.

Ask

For those who ask, there may be no answers;
For those who seek, nothing to be found;
For those who knock, the door may remain shut.

For those who ask, the answers may not be worth having,
Or too much for us to handle;
For those who seek, just the wanting may be better;
For those who knock, the door may only open
To another closed door.

Life is a question, followed by another question;
It is wanting, but not always having;
It is blindness, groping for that
Which is beyond our reach;
Taunting us like the woman with seven veils,
Never allowing us to see, but always daring us
To consider, to ponder, to rage at the winds,
To curse the darkness,
To kick and struggle, rant and rave
With weeping and gnashing of teeth.

Life is the door that won't open,
No matter how hard we knock;
Begging the question of who's on the other side;
If there is someone there who will let us enter
Into the light, into the free?
Or just let us keep raging and beating and
Screaming for entry.
For release into the unknown, beyond the dark vale,
Into the arms of death's warm embrace.

Good Day

Woke up
This morning
This Saturday
Morning
A cartoon
Is on
I don't know which;
Coffee is brewing,
My wife
Is cooking
Sausage biscuits
Again;
Calls me
To the kitchen.
I say, 'What?'
She says,
'I love you,
babe'
I say,
It's gonna
Be
A good day.'

When

When did the love we swore to uphold
Become the hate that consumes us cold?

When did the hand that longed to caress you
Become the fist that threatens to destroy you?

When did I, the lover in your bed,
Become the monster that now looms in your head?

When?

When did the passion you aroused in me
Become the rage that seeks to devour thee?

When did the house wherein dwelt our union
Become the prison you sought to escape?

When did our wedded bliss
Become all this madness?

When?

Nocturnal Emissions

Sax man
In downstairs apartment
Wailing
Like there's no tomorrow
Like he's got the world
On his shoulders
Like,
His woman done him wrong;
Like,
The rent is due
And he's broker
Than broke
(Lord, don't I know
how that is!)

I think Coltrane
Would've liked
This brother—
Blowing blues
'round about
Midnight,
Keeping me awake,
While probably
Lulling others
To sleep;
But I don't mind,
Cause I could use
The accompaniment
As I sit
At the kitchen table
Writing my own blues,
Feeling like,

The world's on my shoulders;
Like,
My woman's done me wrong;
Like,
The rent is due
And I'm broker
Than broke;
Writing like my life
Depended on each word
I write—
Which it probably does.
As the full moon shines
Through the window,
As the sax man
Downstairs
Continues wailing,
Time seems to
Stand still
As I finish
My poem
And all I'm left
With
Is just jazz.

Psalm

Out of the depths
I cry to you, O Lord;
Save me, save me!
From my enemies—
Fear, lust, and doubt, O Lord,
Save me, save me!
Comfort my soul
Life me up, O Lord,
Save me, save me!
Listen to my cry
Turn to me, O Lord,
Save me, save me!
If not you,
Then who, O Lord,
Save me, save me!
Unto you, I commit
My soul, O Lord,
Save me, save me!
My heart, my mind,
My strength, O Lord,
Save me, save me!
All that I am
All that I have, O Lord,
Save me, save me!
Hear my cry,
Comfort my soul,
Stay my enemies, O Lord,
Save me, save me!
If not you,
Then who, O Lord!
Save me, save me!

9-11 Redux

Echoes of F.D.R.
Ring in my head—
"A day which will live
in infamy";
Ringing,
Like the phone
Which awoke
Me from sleep.
Asleep,
While somewhere,
Scores were dying.
And now I find it harder
To sleep
'cause now I hear blood
crying from the ground.

People will ask,
'Do you remember where
you were when?'
And I will say,
'Yeah, in a state of shock,'
which turned into
a New York
state of mind,
wishing I could stop
the madness
that crashed into
the twin brothers
in this first year
of the new century
on the 11th day
of the 9th month—

a day whose numbers
are linked
with the number
for emergency;
a day when chaos ruled
and the news became
a liturgical obituary;

when my bloodshot eyes
were red, not from lack of sleep,
but from the carnage
that filled my TV screen;
when the local news
battled the world news
for body counts.

They say in space,
'No one can hear you scream',
But on this day,
I think I heard
The whole universe
Screaming,
A sound matched only
By the falling of raindrops
In a forest of humanity.

Gratis

You are
the poem
I haven't
written
yet.

Your words
Have shown
Me
How free
I am
To be
Me.

Which is
What
A poem
Should
Do.

Tells us
The
Truth.
Opens
our eyes
Holds
Our hand
Grabs us
By
The throat
Kisses
Our lips

Hugs us
Close
Kicks
Our butt
Reveals
To us
Who
We are.

You
are the
poem
I haven't
written
yet.

Or
maybe
I have.

Or
maybe
you wrote
it
for me.

Thank
You.

The Boy In The Plastic Bubble

The boy in the plastic bubble
Stares back at me, crying,
As I eat my dinner.
And our eyes connect,
Though I don't know how.
And I'm reminded of an 8-year old boy
In a housing project
On the South Side of Chicago,
Who threw up macaroni and cheese
That his stepfather forced him to eat.
And I fast-forward back to now,
Where I sit, glued to my seat,
Staring back at the boy in the plastic bubble.
His image, frozen,
Like my dinner was,
Before I popped it in the oven
At 375 degrees
To cook for 40 minutes,
Because I couldn't afford to go out
And get a real meal.
And I still don't like macaroni and cheese,
Which someone brought over for a potluck,
And didn't bother to take it home with them;
And now I have to throw it out,
Because it's starting to smell
And the smell makes me nauseous.
And yes, I know I'm rambling,
But I can't take my eyes away from
The boy in the plastic bubble,

Staring back at me, crying,
As I eat my dinner;
And then I suddenly realize
That that boy is me
And now I've lost my appetite.

Riding The Coltrane

Meditating on a love supreme—
Riding the "L" past Fullerton and Clark,
Bebop poet with grey dreadlocks
Under a green beret,
Wearing tie-dyed jeans with
An "Oh my God, they killed Kenny" T-shirt on,
Is making his way through my car;
Laying down rhymes
About the passage of time
And how we all still need to get along
Cause we only have one life to live;
And how he'd rather be bold and beautiful,
Than young and restless,
Cause that might land you in a hospital,
General or otherwise;
And how the days of our lives are
But like falling sand in an hourglass,
My children,
For we passengers were all his children
And you see, it's <u>all</u> about loving;
But I digress,
Cause this is supposed to be a jazz poem
And jazz is one part digression
And the rest is all sex and sin
And sax and violins and memories and shit—
The good jazz anyway
And I like good jazz:
Like Lady Day on a rainy night,
And Thelonius in his pork-pie hat,
And Miles cooking up his bitches' brew,
And Coltrane, Coltrane, like this train,
Gliding smooth through that tunnel

Of love, through that tunnel of bullshit
And what the fuck and don't give a damn
About the man who can't see past
The color of my skin to
The content of my character;
Or the woman
Who can't see my forest for the trees;
Gliding, gliding,
Making its way to the downtown
Of my soul,
Like good jazz should,
Making stops along the way,
Picking up passengers
And dropping off others;
Y'all better get on board,
Cause once it takes off,
It may not stop;
And I think I just heard the man yell,
This is the "express" train,
Not the "A" train,
That's up in Harlem;
And we talkin' bout Coltrane,
And not Duke,
For he's the subject
Of a whole 'nother poem
That I ain't wrote yet;
But once again, I digress,
Even though this is supposed to be a jazz poem
And jazz is one part digression
And the rest is all sex and sin
And sax and violins
And memories and shit—
The good jazz anyway
And I like good jazz;
Like Coltrane, Coltrane;
Glide on, Trane, glide on,
Yeah!

A Poem For Nicole

You gave me a glimpse into your world
Through your words and images
Into the heart of a child
Not yet grown,
Not knowing pains and sorrows
Normally reserved for adults.
In your garden of roses and lilies
Are thorns and weeds,
Pricking and suffocating
The innocence which is yours
For being a child.
But fear not,
For the kingdom belongs to one such as you.
Fret not,
For your time will come
And Narnia will be yours to possess.

Until then,
Behold your mother,
For she is wisdom
That will make sense to you
When you are older.
Take her hand,
For she is your fellow pilgrim
On a journey
Through a world of dark closets
That often lead nowhere
And paths
Where angels fear to tread.
Worry not
About things
Which are not yet yours to have,

For they will come soon enough.
Question, yes,
For life is questions,
But if the answers don't come,
Live life anyway,
With all the gusto you can muster
And with the one who made you as you are,
And has given you the keys to His world.

So, cherish these precious moments,
For they will not come again,
And so that you will have no time for regrets.
Carry on, Nicole,
And let no one look down on you
Because of your youth.
Continue writing the poem
That is your life,
For all the world to read.
Let the flame that was ignited
Twelve years ago,
Burn brightly for all the world to see,
For that has been your gift to me,
And, I know the world needs such a gift.
So now, little one,
You who are Nicole,
You who are light like the sun,
I exhort you to rise and…
Shine!!!

Soliloquy (A "Working" Title)

Looking up
While falling down
I see the You
I want to be;
The I AM
That I want to become
And I cry.

Looking in
Instead of out
The null and void
Is crying out
To be filled
With your very essence.
To live, to move,
To have Your being
Become my being.

To cease,
No,
Decrease, so
That you might increase
Yourself
In myself.

What am I
That your mind is full of me?
And You wish to fill mine
With all of You?
I know that to be
Is not to be You—
That is not the question;

But to give up the I am,
For the I AM;
To deny myself
That I might reflect you,
Yea, to become like You,
Is the answer to becoming
The Me you want me
To be.

From A Wandering Stream Of Consciousness

Seize the day!
Gather ye rosebuds while you may;
Suck the very marrow out of life,
All of it.
Feel free to live, to breathe, to move,
To have your being.
Dance among the lilies of the field, yea,
Laugh out loud at the pouring rain,
Shout 'Hallelujah!' to the sun.
For there is a time to every purpose
And a purpose to every rhyme
Or reason—
But I ramble.
Which , of course, is my right to do
Since this is my poem—
My heart's voice crying out
In this wilderness we call life;
Crying out from this huddled mass,
Yearning to breathe free.
Would that I could wander as aimlessly
As this poem has, which of course,
Is my right to do, since this is my poem.

Cool Never Dies

(for Lester Dickens)

I'm crying
Jazz tears
Weeping Miles
Wailing Coltrane
Another Chi-town
Cool breeze
Has passed.
Hipster artist
Old-school
Soul brother
Uncle to
The night--
Has come
And gone;
Stepped off
Into the blue
Leaving memories
Leaving heartache
Leaving town
On the "A" train—
One-way
Express
To peace
Where
Cool never dies.

Nancy, With The Laughing Face

I know Sinatra wasn't singing about her—
This Nancy, with the laughing face;
But her eyes smile at me,
Whenever I walk into a room;
And there's no other place for me to be
Than the cradle of her arms,
Like the baby Jesus and the Virgin Mary,
Though I ain't no baby and she ain't no...
But you get my drift.

Her name means grace,
This Nancy,
With the laughing face;
Her voice, amazing,
How sweet its sound
To this poor wretch,
Saved by her agape love;
By her soft beauty that's made my eyes to see;
I was found by this angel of mercy in sheep's clothing.

Knee to floor, like a knight before his queen,
This Nancy, with the laughing face,
Bids me come—
To partake of sweetest fruits;
To drink honeyed nectars;
To dance among the lilies of the field.
She is the beautiful face of God to me—
A soul seeking sheltered embraces,
Thirsting for love
In a dry and weary land
Where only too few may find it.

And in her arms,
In her embrace,
This Nancy,
With the laughing face,
I find beauty
And I find peace;
She is balm to my Gilead;
And I am changed,
No, not the same;
When she speaks,
Calls out my name;
And I know,
As I am known,
I deserve not
What love has shown
Through this woman of noble race,
Through this Nancy,
With the laughing face.

And then

The neighbors
Upstairs
Are at it again
Yelling and cursing
Cursing and yelling
'he's a bitch'
'she's an asshole'
what can I say?
It's North Hollywood
One of these days
I'm calling
The cops

And then
I hear
A gunshot
And then
I hear
A thud
And then
And then
I hear
A scream
And then
And then
And then…

I'm on
The phone.

Requiem(Good Night, Sweet Princess)

for Diana

The bell has tolled for thee,
But oh too soon, too soon,
And now I mourn for someone I never met.
Though our paths never crossed,
And how could they have,
I still weep as the angels must,
Who now wing you to your final rest.
Away from the hounding, away from the torment,
Away from the shameless vultures
Who stole your image as they stole your life.
For even your life, though royal and precious,
Was held in no regard,
Against the lust of the Almighty dollar
And the 15 seconds of fame.

But your soul, your soul—they'd never touch,
For it was as private to you
As your maternal love was public,
For your children, the world's children.
You, you for whom a fairy tale should not
Have been out of the question.
You, who should have had happy ending
After happy ending.
You, for whom the glass slipper meant nothing
When there were children who had no shoes.
You, who who bit from the bitter apple of life
But yet exuded a sweetness that not even
The sweetest fruit could have matched.

You, sweet princess of Wales,
You, sweet princess of cries and sorrows, too,

Run no more,
Cry no more,
But sleep in heavenly peace.
Sleep, and may your fairy tale now be realized.
Sleep, and may your children grow up to be kings.
Sleep, you who would have been the queen of our hearts.
Sleep, and may the enchanted memory of you
Be burned in our minds.
Sleep.

Looking Through The Glass Menagerie

Blow out your candles, dear Laura
But quench not the flame
That burns within your soul,
Your horn
Which makes you uni-, unique,
Unicorn.
Different from the rest of us
In this glass menagerie—
Where hearts are easily broken
And dreams are easily shattered.

Quasimodo Wept

When you look
At me,
Do you see
Beauty
Or
A beast?

Do you see
A poet
Or
A slave?

Do you see
My heart
Or a pound
Of flesh?

A child of God
Or
A demon
From hell?

A gentleman
Or
A scoundrel?

I've been crucified
For my
Humanness;

Stoned for
Loving
Too deeply;

Vilified for
Speaking truth;

Humiliated for
Lack of
Form and comeliness;

Chastised for
My ability
To bring music
Out of
Noise;
Order
Out of chaos;
Grace out
Of ugliness;
Poetry
Out of
Pain.

For this
I weep;
For this
I shed
Tears;
For this,
I cry out,
'Do you
see me
now?'

Do you
see
me?

Do you
See?

Do you?

Gwendolyn, Gwendolyn

(for Gwendolyn Brooks)

She real cool. She
Old school. She

Wrote truth. She
Fool proof. She

Chi-town. She
Sweet brown. She

Jazz tune. She
Died soon.

Cut, Part 2

The knife
continues
to go deeper
drawing blood
piercing bone
and marrow
stabbing heart
causing disruption
bodily eruption
spiritual corruption
emotional dysfunction
internal combustion

until
the body
is still
breath
a withered vapor
soul eradicated
life evaporated
love annihilated
marriage disintegrated

another hole's
been made
in the eternal ozone layer
disaster
not averted
another homicide
that will go
unsolved
two inner children

reported
missing

but
this story
will not be
televised
not enough
space
in the
newscast
it's not even
fit
for PBS
won't make
the papers
not even
the obituaries

Time would
not allow
for this story
and
it would have
to be
a slow
Newsweek
for this story
to be
printed.

But
that's how
it goes
with some
deaths
not
important enough
for

most human consumption
not
crucial enough
for the
eyes
of the world

the only
acknowledgement
being
the tears
that fall
like rain
from
heaven's keeper.

Mama Said

I was 7 years old
My mama said,
'She didn't need a man',
Or so she said.
She was trying to raise a man.
She came close
With my older brother
And my younger brother
Had a long way to go.
But I was her favorite,
Or so she said.
Though I knew at seven,
Deep down,
She loved us all.
Because she had to
Because the world was in need of men
Who were loved by their mamas,
Or so she said.
And I believed her
Though I was seven.
Because I knew Mama never lied,
Or so she said.

I was 7 years old
And my mama was my hero
Because there was no daddy,
There never was.
Or so Mama said.
But I knew at seven,
That there had to be
Because all the other kids had daddies.
Well, not all of them.

I asked Mama once
About my daddy.
She just told me he was gone.
Not dead, just gone.
‘Didn’t he care about me?’ I asked.
Maybe he did, in his own way,
Is what she said.
And there was nothing more left to say.
And I was out of questions.
Actually, I didn’t want to know anymore
Because Mama hugged me.
Her child, in training to be a man,
Her favorite,
Or so she said.

Cry Of An Anonymous Traveler

Dry bones,
Withered logs,
Somber cacti
Pass me by in slow motion;
I look out
And
I see
Representations of the times
I've hungered
And thirsted for
Your bread and wine.
And I ask,
'How long, O Lord, how long?'

BLACK MAN

Bravery beyond belief
Lover of women and mankind
Ability to see truth behind the lie
Courage to overcome
Knowledge of his heritage
Manhood unequalled
Autonomous, yet willing to share his self
No turning him around.

So

I saw her face
And my heart stopped.
What is it about her beauty that
Chills me so,
Thrills me so,
Haunts me so?

What spell has she cast
That makes me want to—
Love her so,
Hold her so,
Caress her so?

Is it her eyes
That see right through me?
Her lips,
Which long to touch mine,
Or mine hers?
Or is it her hands
That can hold me just right,
When the sun goes down
And the moon lights the night?

So,
What is your name?
What is your claim?
Is your longing the same?
And why are you
So
Beautiful?

Curtain Call

(for Sandy Christopher)

With a kiss
To the hand,
And a wave
Through the air,
She said her
Goodbye.

But I didn't know
It'd be her
Curtain call;
Her final bow;
Her last hurrah;
Her swan song.

Or I would've brought
Flowers;
Or a round of applause
For her stellar performance
Of
Grace under pressure—
For
She did grace this stage
We call
Life
And none performed
Better than she.

With a song on her lips
And a dance to her walk—
She was
Diva personified,

Without
Letting you know so.

And now
The stage is bare—
There will be
No encore;
Though I would
Cry out for one;
All is silent,
A hush
Falls over
This audience
Of one,
Save
For the sound
Of two hands
Clapping:
Mine.

Bravo!

Othello's Deathbed Curse

Loved too well—
Nay, accuse me not.
For I have loved enough
And then some;
But never too well.
For my heart,
Blinded by love,
Fails at discernment—'tis true.
For this crime,
I am most guilty certain;
Punish me most severe.
For the severest penalty
Cannot equal the pains I've suffered
Or loves unrequited;
Nor match the bitter pill
Or sourest medicine
Of unwarranted affection
Or unmerited scorn.

Oh yes, curse the day—
Love made its acquaintance
Of me,
Only to make me a fool;
Or worser yet,
A wretched pawn
With wounded ego
And battered heart.

Oh yes, curse the day
I first set eyes on that
Which is called woman
And felt the first spark of desire,

Only to have it snuffed out
By unrecognized eye
Or unreturned affection.
Oh yes, curse the day
And again, I say, curse,
With ever-fervent zeal,
The day, not that I was born,
But that I have not died,
From Cupid's arrows flung;
Only to have their mission aborted,
Their intent gone astray,
Leaving me naked and ashamed,
Empty of all feeling,
Numb,
Having drained the well of tears dry.

Loved too well, nay,
I have loved well enough,
Only to be haunted time
And time again.
Nay, I repeat the aforementioned curse.
Curse, I say,
Love and all its vile affectations
Or affections, if you will,
Or not, it matters none.

Curse, my already bleeding heart,
For availing itself to be made vulnerable;
Made susceptible to love's deceits
And woman's charms;
I say, curse the woman,
The weaker sex indeed!
Only in stopping short of inflicting pain
Rather with dagger sharp or poison sweet
Or bullet swift;
Than with the pains of scorn or rejection—
Which, in contrast, last the longer
And inflict not death.
Yes, all of this and more,

I say, curse,
And I say it again,
With all that is within me,
Curse!

The Death Of Cupid

I will shed no more tears
Will not celebrate another love song
Or write another love poem;
I will take my heart from my sleeve
And put it back in my pocket,
Where it belongs,
Where it will be safe;
And walk down this road
Much traveled,
All too familiar,
Where other dejected souls know my name
And share my pain;
Where they sing the blues
And play funeral dirges
For the death of Cupid,
That persistent son-of-a-bitch,
Who was never welcomed anyway,
And wouldn't take no
For an answer;
Who now sleeps among
The dead roses
And lilies tramples
Underfoot by those
Of us who are glad
To see him gone.

A Belated Memorial For A Prophet Long Gone

(for James Baldwin)

His flesh became word
And was spoken among us,
Though we esteemed him not.
With nappy head
And frog eyes—
Not exactly an appearance that
Would easily attract someone.
But he spoke with the tongue
Of a fierce angel,
And his pen was a mighty, two-edged
Sword.

He preached the truth,
In love, of course,
For how else could he have done it?
But heard him, we did not,
Like so many of our prophets before him.
He came from among us,
Yet he was not quite like us,
With a soul that epitomized
The dichotomy, the paradox,
The bittersweet wrestle
Within us all--
Black and white,
Angel and devil,
Male and female,
Saint and sinner,
Slave and free.

But like Martin and Malcolm,
His younger brothers

And fellow warriors before him,
He is now free at last,
His soul having found a resting place—
His sword beaten into a plowshare,
He wrestles no more.

A Wish

As the sun set,
I said a wish for you.
I can't tell you
For it may not come true.
But sometime,
When I am with you,
I will whisper it to you
As I say your name—
Mary.

But A Vapor

Hard he fell,
Blindsided by love,
Never knowing what hit him;
Her face sublime,
Her eyes radiant,
Her smile, resonant,
Like a thousand sunshines.
But could he have her?
Would he have her?
Yes, but alas,
Not for long.
For her life would only be,
But a vapor.
Her love, a mere candle flame
That would burn out,
Just as quickly as it was lit.
Ah, but such is life.
And such is love.
Temporal,
A game played by foolish mortals.
Oh, but how sweet the foolishness!

Lifetime Resolutions (A Work-In-Progress)

Resolved:
To understand that which is still not clear to me.
Resolved:
To live the questions that will not be answered.
Resolved:
To dance to the music that plagues my soul.
Resolved:
To speak the bitter, unspeakable truth.
Resolved:
To see a world in a grain of sand and heaven in a wildflower.
Resolved:
To hear the whispers of a sometimes silent God.
Resolved:
To feel the unavoidable, painful embrace of humanness.
Resolved:
To touch the inner/outer extremities of my soul lover.
Resolved:
To know the why of the rage inside.
Resolved:
To quench the insatiable thirst of my heart and soul.
Resolved:
To walk a mile, maybe more, in my brother's shoes.
Resolved:
To love beyond the limitations of my imagination.
Resolved:
To stand for something other than the reason to sit still no longer.
Resolved:
To read the words of those who probably know more than I do.
Resolved:
To write an end to this still-evolving poem.

Share

Share with me
Share joy
Share a child's laughter
Share smiles
Share a summer day
And a gentle breeze
A walk in the park
And autumn leaves
Share yourself.

Share with me
Share hope
Of eternal bliss
A lover's kiss
A sweet embrace
Your lovely face
Amazing grace
Come,
Share with me.

Share with me
Share love
If necessary,
Use words
But do share.

Share with me
Share music
Share psalms, hymns, and spiritual songs
Share a Dylan tune
A Sinatra croon
A Dizzy beat

Or a piano suite;
Chopin, if you prefer
Or Thelonious—
That's straight, no chaser.

Share with me
Share your dreams
Share the who you are
And hope to be
Share with me.
Share the now and the not yet.
Share your time—
Pacific, Mountain, Central, or Eastern
But share with me.

Share with me
Share your pain
Share the hurt you feel
Share your fear
Share your doubts of God
And doubts of self
Share your burdens
Share the weight of your existence
Share your longings
Share your soul
Share your life with mine
And mine with yours
Share with me.

Withdrawn

He dies a little
each day,
withering on
the vine
of his own
existence
that he'd
hoped
would bear fruit,
only to see
that
it has rotted
to the core.

He thinks
love is a theory
that sounds
good
on paper,
that
should be
lit
by a
match
and
set ablaze.

He drinks
whiskey
from a
water bottle
he keeps

hidden
underneath the
kitchen sink;

watches porno
on the
living room TV
while his wife
sleeps
in the
other room;

thinks sex
is always
better
when
other people
are doing
it
especially
in Technicolor;

hopes death
withdraws
him quickly
from
the hollowness
of a marriage
already
withdrawn.

Of Austin, TX, Billie Holiday, and Peter Paul Rubens

It's her face
I remember;
The light
of the Austin sun
reflected in
her smile;
Her hair,
a golden mane,
crowning
this earthly angel.

She sang
to me,
"Good Morning Heartache"
like Billie Holiday
that made
my heart
ache
with longing
just to
hear it.

And her body,
voluptuous,
sumptuous,
as if
Rubens
had made
one of
his creations
come to
life.

She was
my moonlight serenade
as we
celebrated
an
April night
in
the Paris
of
our minds,
our interlocked souls
and
intertwined bodies--
she,
breaking me
of
my virgin shell,
making me
feel
like a
love poem
I could
never write.

She is
the
beautiful memory
that
haunts me
even now
five years
hence
upon
my return
to that
city
of music
and poetry
where

heartache
welcomes me
home
and
bids me
sit down.

A Reluctant Eulogy

(for Michael Edmonds)

This is for my fallen comrade,
for my brother-in-arms,
for my partner in crime.

I am crying copious tears that
I never expected to shed---
So soon, too soon.

I am not asking God to answer me why
He took my friend,
for I don't expect Him to tell me;

but I am asking Him to turn back the sun
for at least one time,
for one more day to hear his laugh,
for one more day to see that mischievous twinkle in his eye,
for one more day to see that "shit-eating grin".

But I don't expect Him to do that either.

But in time, I hope He will strengthen my fragile memories,
let me hear his laughter in my head,
let me turn those tears into twinkles in my own eyes,
let me wear that "shit-eating grin" that he loved so much,
as I remember the bond we shared
as comrades in the struggle,
as brothers-in-arms,
as partners in crime.

In closing, I will ask of God one thing I expect He will grant—

that I not forget.

Cucumber Melon

My baby loves cucumber melon—
Like fresh dew on a summer morning,
Like wet kisses under a moonlit sky,
Like the afterglow from making love;
My baby loves cucumber melon.

My baby loves cucumber melon—
Like Coltrane and "A Love Supreme";
Like "April in Paris";
Like a "Moonlight Serenade";
My baby loves cucumber melon.

My baby loves cucumber melon—
Like when your lover calls your name;
Like apple pie a la mode;
Like the sound of a baby's laughter;
My baby loves cucumber melon.

My baby loves cucumber melon—
Like a sonnet in iambic pentameter;
Like a kickass haiku;
Like a love poem by a gray-haired poet;
My baby loves cucumber melon.

My baby loves cucumber melon—
Like a bouquet of fresh roses;
Like the taste of sweet wine;
Like the words, 'I love you';
My baby loves cucumber melon.

Barack Means Blessed

When Jesse said, "I am, Somebody",
He was talking about this one;
When JB said it loud...,
He was talking about this one;
The shining black prince, that was Malcolm,
And the gentle warrior, that was Martin--
Have come back to us
As this fortunate one,
This fortunate son;
The African diaspora and the American dream,
Clothed in this one man,
In this man,
Blessed by God,
For that is what Barack means.
This man,
Standing on the shoulders
Of those who came before,
Both great and small,
Black and white;
This man,
This human,
Jazzman,
Michelle's, Malia's, and Sasha's man,
Our man
For these times,
These interesting times;
Courageous,
Audacious;
Proud,
Yet humbled;
Black
And beautiful;

A leader
And yet,
A servant.

This one,
This man,
Renaissance man,
Helping us to see
What it means,
To be reborn;
Helping us to see
What it means,
As a people,
As a nation,
As these United States of America,
To be blessed by God,
For that is what Barack means.

Prodigal

I remember the sound of joyful noise
When I cried out your name,
The smell of your perfume;
The tears I shed
As I laid my head
At your feet.

I remember the smile on my face
As you spoke my name,
As if I was just hearing it
For the first time.

I remember,
Lord, do I remember,
Though your name rarely crosses
My lips anymore;
My eyes are dry,
And your fragrance,
A distant memory.

And the noise I hear now,
Are the voices,
The voices,
Coming at me from all directions,
From within
And without,
Deafening,
Deafening.

And yet,
And yet,
They do not drown out

What I remember
Of you;
That which has brought me,
Stumbling,
To your doorstep,
For another whiff of your perfume,
To hear you say my name,
To lay my head at your feet;
Because I'm afraid,
I might not remember
For long.

Don't Say Goodbye, Just Leave

When the love has gone
And the sun becomes
A dark cloud in the sky
Don't say goodbye,
Just leave.

When the promises you make,
You break
And the truth
Becomes a lie,
Don't say goodbye,
Just leave.

If the tears in my eyes,
No longer make you cry,
Don't say goodbye,
Just leave.

When the heart that you swore,
Chooses to walk out the door,
Don't say goodbye,
Just leave.

If you happen to find another
Whom you think a better lover
Don't say goodbye,
Just leave.

DEF POET

If I were a slam poet
and, I'm not, by the way,
I'd breathe similes
into your nostrils
and give you life;
(w)rap metaphors
around your ears
like the garland wrapped
in Billie Holiday's hair;
I would not lull you
to sleep,
because my words
would be on fire,
shocking you
with
existential soliloquies,
like,
to be
or not to be;
making you
hear songs
in the key of life;
making you
hear rhapsodies
in the key of blue,
if I were a slam poet.

If I were a slam poet,
in three minutes or less,
I'd fire word darts
into your mind,
fire projectile missiles

of poetic wisdom,
like a sermon on the mount
in iambic pentameter;
spin romantic sonnets
that would have made
Shakespeare jealous;
from behind the mike,
my words
would spring forth
like an Ellington tune,
played by Miles Davis,
alongside John Coltrane,
backed by Thelonius Monk,
and Charles Mingus;
like your mama's voice,
when the hurt was so bad
and nobody else's words would do;
make you recall memories
you'd long forgotten;
recall memories
you wish you had;
makin' those three minutes,
a memory
that you will
never forget--
that is,
if I were a slam poet,
which,
I'm not.

Blessed Union Of Souls

Dearly beloved,
We are gathered today
To celebrate
This blessed union of souls;
This blessed union
Of a man
To a woman and child;
Of a husband to a wife,
Of a daughter to a want-to-be,
Hoped-to-be,
Promise-to-be,
Father.

Witness, if you please,
The pledges of love here today;
A thing of beauty
That will be a joy forever.
Acknowledge, if you will,
This blessed trinity,
This family;
Assure and affirm them, with
Your loyalty and devotion
As they commit to each other
Their loyalty and devotion;
Assure them of your presence
In their lives--
That they will be upheld
By strong arms of love and support;
That the ties that bind
Will never be severed.

Affirm them in their uniqueness,

Their beautiful blend,
Their wonderful eclectic mixture
Of color and spirit,
Of love and peace;
Again, I say, a thing of beauty.

Behold, Toni, Joseph, and Santi,
These three,
These precious three
As they become one,
As they become a symbol
Of what God can do.

So elevate,
Appreciate,
Celebrate,
This blessed union of souls,
This trinity of love and devotion,
This family.

MJJ

The silence
has never been
more deafening;
the man in the mirror
is now crying,
as a single white glove
falls to the floor;
while
a child in Ethiopia
is putting on
dance shoes
someone gave him
as a gift;
and a child in Harlem
is about to
take the stage
to belt his heart out
to a crowd
that spills out
into the street;
and a child,
a stone's throw
from where I grew up,
where I learned about
ABC's,
and about saving love---
looks up
and sees
a shooting star
streaking across
the night sky.

Mofo' Risin'

The beautiful
Fucked-up man
Has left
The
Building
And he's
Taken his
Cross,
What's left
Of his
Dignity
And manhood
And his
Creamy
Peanut butter,
Because
Only choosy
Motherfuckers
Choose creamy
Peanut butter,
Jif or otherwise.

And
he's going
to devote
himself
to his
poetry
because
only real
motherfuckin' men
write poetry.

And he's
Going
to devote
himself
to being
a friend
to his friends
and being
a friend
to those
who need
friends
because
only real
motherfuckin' men
are true friends.

And he's
Going
To devote himself
To finding
A woman
Who
Thinks that
He is
Much of
A man
And can
Be
Much of
A husband
Because
Only real
Motherfuckin' men
Know
How to be
Husbands
Even
If they

Have to
Learn
By
Trial and
Error
And by
Fucking up
And trying
Again
And again
Because
They never
Had a
Real
Motherfuckin' man
To
Show them
How
To be
A real
Motherfuckin' man
And how
It would
Take a real
Motherfuckin' woman
To
Understand that
And
Give
A real
Motherfucker
A chance.

But,
In the meantime,
This beautiful
Fucked-up man
Will rise
Up,

Dust himself
Off
And
Move on
With his cross
To bear,
What's left
Of his
Dignity
And manhood
Intact
And his
Creamy
Peanut butter,
Because
Only choosy
Motherfuckers
Choose creamy
Peanut butter.

Be on
The lookout
For him;
He might
Be
A good friend
To you;
He could
Be your
Next lover
Or husband;
Or
He might
Just read
You
This poem
And
Make you
A sandwich

Because
That's what
Real
Motherfuckin' men
Do.

A Freak's Blues

They think
I don't know
That they
talk about
me
behind my back
Or
they don't care.
And it
doesn't matter
Really.
I am
what
I am
A freak
without form
or
comeliness
that others
would
be attracted to;
An anomaly
of God's;
the subject
of
books written
by the likes of
Hugo and Shelley;
An abomination
in the eyes
of those
who would

deem themselves
beautiful.

Hideous,
unknowable,
unlovable,
what fair
creature
would ever
dare
to discover
the love
I possess
in my
heart;
the sorrow
that grips
my soul;
the anguish
that haunts
my dreams;
would dare
to look
past
the ugliness
to see
the saint
within;
the kindly lover;
the passionate poet;
the real beauty
of me.

I believe
heaven
weeps for
those
who are deemed
unworthy

of love,
unworthy
of knowing
as
I stand
in the
shadows
and await
those tears
to
fall and
comfort me.

Just As I Am

Do not look to me for perfection
For I am not perfect;
Do not expect from me forever,
For it has not ever been promised to me;
But look to the God whom I serve,
Who is perfection and,
Who is forever,
And ask Him to help you
Accept me as I am.

Bliss

You are my bliss
Let me follow you
The honey of your kiss
Let me swallow you;
The caress of your fingertips,
Let me feel you;
Your heart, your soul,
Let me steal you.
As your eyes gaze into mine,
Let me see the love
That will not let me go.

From your lips,
Let loose words that will engulf me
In waves of passion unstoppable;
Let our bodies unite as we complete
The circle of that
Which was meant to be
Since the dawn of time
As we enter eternity,
Spinning into infinity;
Losing ourselves and yet,
Finding ourselves,
Changing and growing,
Becoming a glorious one.
Like a phoenix rising,
Spinning and spinning
In a beautiful rapture;
In unmatchable ecstasy,
In sweet copulation,
Like Eros and Psyche,
As we dance to the music of the spheres.

Thoughts Turn To Earl

(On Your 40th Birthday)

My brother,
Soul brother
#1
In my book;
Childhood best
Friend--
Head taller,
Heart stronger;
Had me
By a year.
You were Batman
To my Robin,
In next door yard--
Our field of dreams.
You had the girls,
But I made you laugh.
My inspiration
For being a writer,
For becoming a man,
Though we didn't know
it at the time.
Then,
it was about comic books
and sneakin' into movies;
Dreams of workin' the rails
and seeing the sights;
Of
endless summer days
and mystery theater nights,
and the radio show
that would've been
a hit

if we had been
old enough.
And like Stevie sang,
I wish
those days
could
come back
once more,
why did
those days
ever
have to go.
And I flash
to the present
and wonder
where you are
and how you are,
my forever
brother,
and if
your thoughts
ever
turn to me.

Lo, How Two Roses Not Yet Blooming

(for Martin and Marvin)

On this day in April
I saw two roses,
not quite in full bloom
just yet,
fall to the ground.
And cried
blood-red tears.
Screamed,
'What's going on?'
Wailed,
'How long?'
Why do the good
always die young?
Always at the hand
Of those who don't understand
or who have not ears to hear
or eyes to see
beauty
and truth
in flesh beholden.
Even God must weep,
I hope,
for creation yet incomplete,
interrupted,
is most assuredly
a tragedy,
for which
there are never enough tears,
blood-red or otherwise
and all we are left with

after the crying and the weeping
is the remembering
and wondering
what might have been?

A Poet's Life

The pen
And
the page

the mike
and
the stage

the sacred
and
profane

the yin
and
the yang

the love
and
the lust

the fear
and
the trust

such
is
a
poet's life.

Darkness Before Dawn

(A Vampire's Soliloquy)

If I told you
I had lustful thoughts,
Would that shock you?
A thirst for blood
That has nothing to do
With revenge.
Mine is a divided soul
And I've given in
To its darker side
Because the light
Just doesn't do it for me
Anymore.

I prowl the streets at night,
Savoring the darkness;
Looking to satiate my hunger,
Knowing it will never be satisfied.
I lie in wait
And bide my time,
For one who's unfortunate enough
To cross my path,
For one who will be my prey—
Just for tonight,
Just for this night…

I strike!

I Know What It Means To Miss New Orleans

French Quarter
Bourbon Street and cool jazz
Cheap beer, 7 & 7's,
And hot sex in
Third story hotel window.
Dive bars and cable cars
Beads, blues, and voodoo
And Kermit Ruffin,
A modern-day Satchmo,
Tearin' it up
At the Blue Nile.

Everybody tryin'
To make a buck or two;
Some of them tryin'
To take a buck from you;
Sometimes, we say,
'What the fuck?'—
voodoo!
Night is day
And day never seems to end.
What happens here,
Doesn't necessarily
Have to stay here,
For you have to take
Your memories with you
When you check out.
You don't have to leave,
But if you do stay,
It's gonna cost you
More than you know,
More than you know.

Family Snapshots

Snapshot #1

I've traded in my tears of solitude
for the love of a good woman
and a child who chooses
to call me father---
I am doubly blessed,
though I never expected it
and never knew how to look for it;
yet I receive them
as I would a precious gift,
beautifully wrapped,
presented in love,
not to own, so much,
but to cherish
and enjoy in their splendor.

Snapshot #2

She calls me husband
And I will do my damnedest
to aspire to be that;
And going in,
I know I will fail
and fail many times,
for I am not perfect;
but it is not perfection
I seek,
at least,
not in her eyes;
what I seek,

is to be
what she calls me---
husband.

Snapshot #3

I will call her wife
And I will do my damnedest
to help her to be that---
not on a pedestal,
not walking behind me,
but partner,
at my side,
for life.

I will seek
to allow her beauty
to shine,
as the precious ruby
that I have found;

I will make room
for her voice
to be heard,
for her voice
will not be contained.

I will call her wife---
partner at my side,
partner of my life,

I will call her wife.

Snapshot #4

Her name is Santi,
which means peace--
And peace is what

she brings to me;
but I will choose
to call her
daughter,
for that is what
she is to me;
though she is not
of my blood,
though I was not
present
at her birth,
and I did not
watch her grow,
as one would watch
seeds and buds
grow into flowers;
I will still
call her
daughter
and be present
as that flower
continues to burst
into bloom,
bringing peace
to others.

Snapshot #5

This family you celebrate
here tonight,
is just one verse
of a larger poem
that continues
to be written;
you friends,
are other verses,
that when added,
will make that poem sing.

So ask yourself,
what verse
will you contribute?
What is the poem
that you want this family
to be?

And then,
go
and write it!

I Am Black History

My life is black history. The very fact that I exist. My mama's son. Third of five. Didn't know my father. Wanting to be a father. Wanting to be a man, wanting to be a writer—wanting to be James Baldwin, Langston Hughes, Maya Angelou, the entire Harlem Renaissance wrapped up in one. Standing on the shoulders of those who came before, who kicked down the door, so that I could strut right through, doing the funky chicken and the jitterbug, to Duke's "A-train", and Miles' "Kind of Blue".

My life is black history. Growing up in high-rise projects. Fat kid with four eyes and crooked teeth. The brain, the Professor, they called me. And sometimes it's hard to hold your nappy head up, sometimes it's hard to press on, wondering what it means to overcome, just trying to stay in school and keep mama from "whuppin' your behind". Playing in rundown yards and broken down cars, dreaming you were someone else, like the Batman, sometimes dreaming you lived somewhere else, anywhere but where you lived.

My life is black history, but the kind that is still ongoing, that still lives and moves and has its being. The kind that says I can, as one man, make a difference, again like those who came before, especially the ones who aren't in the history books. You can't tell me my history—the reason we aren't in the history books, is because it would take more books than we know what to do with to tell our story-- his story, her story, my story.

My life is a song of my people, black people, black and beautiful, black and proud. It is a love poem, to my mama, about my mama, in celebration of my mama—of all mamas. It's also a love poem to my brothers and my sisters, and to my 'bruthas' and 'sistahs'. It's a thank you for wiping my nose and kicking my ass, for giving me wisdom and helping me grow, for showing me God and how to dance with the devil. For the blues and funk. For poetry and the telling of our stories. For teaching me to appreciate myself without having to look down on others, regardless of race, color, or creed.

My life is black history, in all its glorious splendor. The man that I am and still want to be; the lover of my woman that I still aspire to be; the poet and writer, the preacher and the teacher, instilled in me, still yearning to display himself for the world, "for him who has ears to hear". I share with you my life, my history, but you must accept it on its own terms and not what you wish to make it, for it will not be denied, like the shining of the

sun or the brightness of the moon. My life is history in the making, my life is black history.

Words

In deepest shadows
In darkest void
A voice comes to me in the night
Speaking light into being
Talking truth
Screaming beatitudes
Whispering love songs
Illuminating that which I couldn't understand
Stripping away the mystery
Of all that I beheld in finitude
Calming my storms
Soothing the savage beast of my soul
Conveying the unmistakable
Leaving me with poetry
Leaving me with:
Words that gave me life,
Words that saved my life,
Words that are my life.

Manifesto-Why I Write

Because I must;
Because I can;
Because it's akin to breathing
And the alternative is unthinkable.
Because the love of Christ compels me.
Because the love of mankind compels me.
Because, sometimes, I can never say what I feel.
Because the truth needs to be read
And newspapers are slowly going out of business.

Because a 10-year old black boy,
on the South Side of Chicago,
wearing glasses, chubby and
with crooked teeth,
needs to know it's possible.

Because a 40-ish white writer I met
at an art show near downtown L.A. the other night,
needs to know it's possible
and needs to give a shit
and come out from his shell.

Because I'm getting better at it, even though
no one pays me a dime for it.

Because James Baldwin did it.
And Langston Hughes did it.
And Gwendolyn Brooks did it.
And so did Maya Angelou.

Because it's the closest I'll ever come
to singing.
Because it's the closest I'm ever going to come
to playing jazz. And I love jazz!

Because I still have stuff to say, even if
I don't know what that is just yet.

Because being a writer
is the best thing in the world,
second only to being a teacher...
Or maybe a firefighter...
Or maybe even a cop...
Or a doctor, but that's it.

Because, aside from never recognizing
another person's talent, it's a damn shame
to allow one's talent to be squandered;
for one's light to be hidden;
a gift to be kept to one's self;
for words to never be written, even if
they've been written before.

And that is why I write.

ABOUT THE AUTHOR

Joseph Powell is the author of four chapbooks of poetry, including "Blood On The Page" and "Mofo' Risin' "; he was also a featured poet in the National Geographic/PBS documentary, "Skin". He currently lives in Burbank, California with his wife, Toni, stepdaughter, Santi, and two chihuahuas, Monty and Mishibean

www.ingramcontent.com/pod-product-compliance
Ingram Content Group UK Ltd.
Pitfield, Milton Keynes, MK11 3LW, UK
UKHW040602210726
13854UKWH00008B/1714

9 780557 104246